Important Work

By T. J. Cox

Illlustrated by Johanna Westerman

Angela and Tom volunteer at a food bank on Saturdays. The food bank gives food, such as fruit and bread, to people who cannot buy it.

Every Saturday Angela, Tom, and Angela's mom go to a local market where farmers sell fruit and vegetables. They always arrive 15 minutes before the market closes. But they don't buy anything. They urge farmers to give their surplus food to the food bank.

Angela and Tom talk to a farmer about the food he did not sell that day.

"If these fruits and vegetables are not eaten soon, they will have to be thrown away," says Tom.

Angela says, "This wonderful food should not become garbage. It's wasteful."

The children tell the farmer how his fruit and vegetables would be useful to the food bank.

"Many people are hungry," Tom says.

"And they will be thankful for the good food," says Angela.

The children are successful. The farmer agrees to give them his extra food.

"How can I argue about helping people?" he asks. "What you are doing is wonderful. Return next week. I'll give you everything I have not sold."

Later Angela and Tom get more food from the other farmers at the market. It is a really good day. They get hundreds of pounds of free food from the farmers.

Angela, Tom, and Angela's mom carefully pack the fruits and vegetables into cartons. Then they load the boxes on their truck and go to the food bank.

Other workers at the food bank help Angela and Tom. They unload the food, sort it, and put it into bags. The bags of food are given to people who cannot afford groceries. One person gets three bags. A larger family gets more bags.

The farmers at the market gave Angela and Tom a lot of fruit and vegetables. But the food bank needs more food. The workers and helpers are always looking for places with available food.

They ask restaurants and grocery stores for older but still acceptable food. The workers put the food into refrigerated trucks. After it gets to the food bank, it is refrigerated again. Then it is packed into bags and given to people.

There are many large fruit orchards and vegetable gardens in the area. But people pick only the largest fruits and vegetables there. Many small fruits and vegetables are left behind.

Angela and Tom asked the owners of the orchards if they could gather this food for the food bank. The owners thought it was a clever idea. Every week many people meet at a garden or orchard to collect food.

Angela, Tom, and the other workers prepare the bags of food. Soon people will come to the food bank and get their food.

Working at the food bank takes a lot of time and work. Angela and Tom aren't paid for their work. They don't get any prizes or medals. But they don't mind. They don't want money or awards. Like volunteers all over the world, they help others because it's the right thing to do.